U.S.A. TRAVEL GUIDES

CONNECTICUT

BY ANN HEINRICHS • ILLUSTRATED BY MATT KANIA

The Child's World®
childsworld.com

Published by The Child's World®
1980 Lookout Drive • Mankato, MN 56003-1705
800-599-READ • www.childsworld.com

ISBN 9781503819474
LCCN 2016961124

Printing
Printed in the United States of America
PA02334

Ann Heinrichs is the author of more than 100 books for children and young adults. She has also enjoyed successful careers as a children's book editor and an advertising copywriter. Ann grew up in Fort Smith, Arkansas, and lives in Chicago, Illinois.

post card

About the Author
Ann Heinrichs

Matt Kania loves maps and, as a kid, dreamed of making them. In school he studied geography and cartography, and today he makes maps for a living. Matt's favorite thing about drawing maps is learning about the places they represent. Many of the maps he has created can be found in books, magazines, videos, Web sites, and public places.

post card

About the
Map Illustrator
Matt Kania

On the cover: Sail along the coast of New London.

OUR CONNECTICUT TRIP

CONNECTICUT

What's going on in Connecticut today? Let's take a tour and see! You'll find plenty to explore there.

You'll wander through whaling ships and submarines. You'll see dinosaurs, beaver homes, and donkey shows. You'll watch giant balloons floating down the street. And you'll meet Mark Twain and Nathan Hale. Not bad for such a tiny state!

Are you ready to roll? Then buckle up and hang on tight. We're off to see Connecticut!

WELCOME TO
CONNECTICUT

Connecticut's Nicknames: The Constitution State, the Nutmeg State, and the Provision State

MASSACHUSETTS

NEW YORK

North Canaan

As you travel through Connecticut, watch for all the interesting facts along the way.

Burlington

Hartford

Brooklyn

Bristol

CONNECTICUT

Willimantic

RHODE ISLAND

Connecticut River

Mashantucket

Ridgefield

New Haven

Essex

Groton • Mystic

95

Stamford

Long Island Sound

NEW YORK

ATLANTIC OCEAN

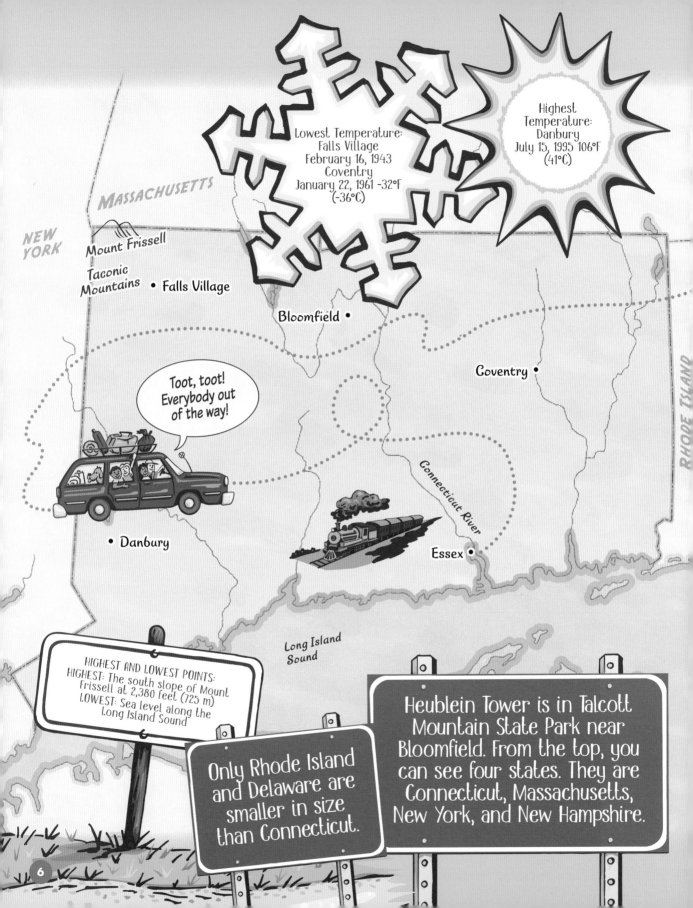

Lowest Temperature:
Falls Village
February 16, 1943
Coventry
January 22, 1961 -32°F
(-36°C)

Highest
Temperature:
Danbury
July 15, 1995 106°F
(41°C)

MASSACHUSETTS

NEW YORK

Mount Frissell

Taconic Mountains • Falls Village

Bloomfield •

Coventry •

RHODE ISLAND

Toot, toot! Everybody out of the way!

Connecticut River

• Danbury

Essex •

Long Island Sound

HIGHEST AND LOWEST POINTS:
HIGHEST: The south slope of Mount Frissell at 2,380 feet (725 m)
LOWEST: Sea level along the Long Island Sound

Only Rhode Island and Delaware are smaller in size than Connecticut.

Heublein Tower is in Talcott Mountain State Park near Bloomfield. From the top, you can see four states. They are Connecticut, Massachusetts, New York, and New Hampshire.

RIDING THE ESSEX STEAM TRAIN

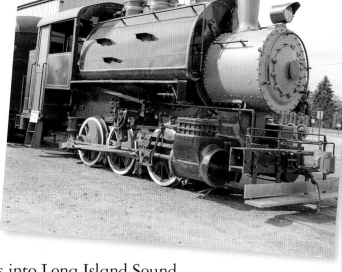

All aboard for the Essex Steam Train! Puffy steam clouds pour from the smokestack. Soon you're chugging through the countryside. What a way to explore the Connecticut River Valley!

The Connecticut River flows through central Connecticut. It empties into Long Island Sound. That's part of the Atlantic Ocean. Connecticut's whole southern border is a seacoast. Fishing and sailing are big parts of Connecticut's history.

Much of Connecticut is hilly. Deep river valleys cut through the hills. The Taconic Mountains reach into northwest Connecticut. This is the state's highest region. The land here is wild and rugged.

The Essex Steam Train travels through meadows, by a waterfall, and over bridges.

WILDLIFE AT SESSIONS WOODS

Have you ever seen a beaver lodge? Just visit Sessions Woods Wildlife Management Area. It's near Burlington. You'll see amazing, cone-shaped beaver houses. Beavers build them with sticks, grass, and mud.

Keep wandering through the woods. You'll see chipmunks, turtles, and frogs. You'll meet some white-tailed deer, too.

Many animals make their homes in Connecticut's forests. They include foxes, skunks, rabbits, and raccoons. Sometimes a snowy owl hoots in the trees.

Gulls, sandpipers, and terns live by the shore. Plenty of shellfish live offshore, too. There are clams, oysters, scallops, and lobsters. People love to eat them!

Keep an eye out for beavers at Sessions Woods!

STATE BIRD:
AMERICAN ROBIN

STATE FLOWER:
MOUNTAIN LAUREL

STATE TREE:
CHARTER OAK (WHITE OAK)

MASSACHUSETTS

NEW YORK

• Burlington

Watch those beavers! They go underwater to get into their houses.

RHODE ISLAND

You'll learn about all kinds of sea life at Mystic Aquarium and Institute for Exploration.

Mystic •

ATLANTIC OCEAN

Long Island Sound

Black bears live in Connecticut. They have five toes on each foot. Males are called boars, and females are sows.

The National Park Service has five sites in Connecticut.

Who Lived Here before Europeans Arrived? Mohegan, Niantic, Paugusset, Pequot, Eansketambawg, Saukiog, Siwanoy, Tunxis, and Wangunk

New Haven formed a separate colony in 1638. It joined the Connecticut Colony in 1665.

MASSACHUSETTS

NEW YORK

RHODE ISLAND

Windsor •

• Washington

Mashantucket •

The Pequot still live in Connecticut today.

New Haven •

Long Island Sound

The Institute for American Indian Studies is in Washington. It includes a 1600s Algonquin village.

Connecticut colonists adopted the Fundamental Orders in 1639. This was a type of constitution, or basic set of laws. That's why Connecticut is called the Constitution State.

Hey, look! The Pequot played a game called hubbub. It's sort of like playing with two-sided dice.

MASHANTUCKET PEQUOT MUSEUM

Stroll through Mashantucket Pequot Museum. Its life-size scenes teach visitors about the Pequot culture. The Pequot people have lived in Connecticut for hundreds of years. You'll learn how they built homes and canoes. You'll see how they cooked, hunted, and played.

Museum exhibits show how Native Americans' lives changed when settlers arrived. Dutch and English settlers were Connecticut's first Europeans. The English founded Windsor that same year. Windsor and other new towns formed the Connecticut **Colony**. It was one of England's thirteen American colonies.

Early **colonists** were farmers. Some also hunted and fished for food. Manufacturing began as early as the 1700s. Connecticut factories made clocks, ships, and silver goods.

You'll see many canoes at the Mashantucket Pequot Museum. The Pequot relied on canoes for fishing and transportation.

RIDGEFIELD'S KEELER TAVERN AND THE REVOLUTIONARY WAR

In time, colonists grew sick of British rule. They decided to fight for their freedom. They fought the British in the Revolutionary War (1775–1783). Nathan Hale of Connecticut was a war hero.

One battle took place in Ridgefield. The British shot at Keeler **Tavern**. A British cannonball is still stuck there! Just stop by, and you can see it. That tavern is now a museum. The museum's guides wear colonial clothing.

How did the war turn out? The colonists won! Then the colonies became the first thirteen states.

Be sure to visit the beautiful gardens at Keeler Tavern!

Connecticut was the fifth state to enter the Union. It joined on January 9, 1788.

MASSACHUSETTS

NEW YORK

RHODE ISLAND

Nathan Hale is Connecticut's official state hero.

The Battle of Ridgefield took place on April 27, 1777.

• Ridgefield

Fort Griswold Battlefield is in Groton. British troops beat Americans there in 1781.

New London •
• Groton

Dear Mr. Hale:
The British hanged you for being a spy. You were only 21 years old. You were proud to die for your homeland. You were very brave.

Sincerely,
A. Patriot

post card

Mr. Nathan Hale
1755-776
New London, CT

British people come from the United Kingdom.

13

Dear Mr. Whitney:
You saw that some goods are made of many parts. Then you had a great idea. Each part should always be the same size. This really sped things up in factories!

Gratefully yours,
Man U. Facturing

Eli Whitney
1765-1825
Hamden, CT

Look at that frog statue! It's sitting on top of a spool of thread. The frog is Willimantic's official animal.

MASSACHUSETTS

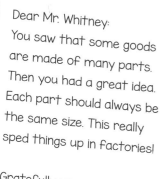

The Mill Museum's full name is the Windham Textile and History Museum.

• Willimantic

RHODE ISLAND

NEW YORK

• Hamden

Long Island Sound

The American Thread Company was in Willimantic. The city's nickname is Thread City.

Mills that stood alongside a river used flowing water to turn a mill wheel. That powered the mills' machine parts.

THE MILL MUSEUM IN WILLIMANTIC

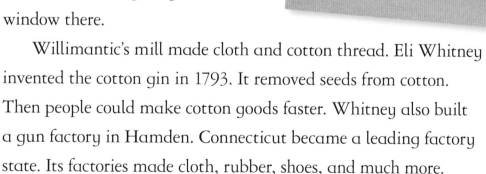

Roam around the Mill Museum. You'll begin to see how mill workers lived. Mills were early factories. People worked there 12 or more hours a day. Even children worked in the mills.

You'll see a mill worker's house. You'll also see the supervisor's office. The supervisor would watch the workers through a glass window there.

Willimantic's mill made cloth and cotton thread. Eli Whitney invented the cotton gin in 1793. It removed seeds from cotton. Then people could make cotton goods faster. Whitney also built a gun factory in Hamden. Connecticut became a leading factory state. Its factories made cloth, rubber, shoes, and much more.

At the Windham Textile and History Museum, you'll find out what life was like in Connecticut's 1890s textile mill towns.

RIVERFRONT DRAGON BOAT & ASIAN FESTIVAL IN HARTFORD

Join the fun at the Riverfront Dragon Boat and Asian Festival. You can watch a dragon boat race. The event is originally from China. The boats look like dragons! Twenty people paddle a boat. A drummer sits in the front of the boat. The paddlers paddle to the beat of the drum. One person in back steers the boat.

This festival celebrates Asian culture. Enjoy a Kung Fu demonstration. Listen to the rhythms of Japanese taiko drums. Then eat lots of Asian food!

In 2015, about 1 out of every 20 people in Connecticut was Asian. People from many other regions have come to Connecticut, too. Early settlers were from England. Many **immigrants** came to work in the mills. Some arrived from Ireland or Canada. Others came from Italy, Poland, Germany, or Russia. They all made new homes in Connecticut.

Dragon boats race on the Connecticut River.

The steerperson steers a dragon boat. A really good steerperson can steer without putting the oar in the water!

In 2016, 3,576,452 people lived in Connecticut. It's the 29th largest state by population.

NEW YORK

Uthappam is a South Indian pancake. It is made with rice and lentils. Toppings can include onion, ginger, cilantro, carrots, and more!

Hartford

Canterbury

RHODE ISLAND

Connecticut River

• New Haven

POPULATION OF LARGEST CITIES
Bridgeport.....................147,629
New Haven.....................130,322
Hartford.....................124,006

• Bridgeport

Long Island Sound

People from Finland came to Connecticut in the 1920s. Many settled in the Canterbury area.

What time is it? Just look around. You'll see what time it is—5,500 times! You're at the American Clock and Watch Museum.

This museum has more than 5,500 clocks and watches. You'll see grandfather clocks. You'll see clocks for shelves and walls. There is a clock that looks like a chef, too. Check out the museum's oldest timepiece. It was made in 1630!

Some clocks used to be in factories. They punched the workers' "in and out" times. Other clocks came from railroad stations or church towers. On the hour, you'll get to hear all the chimes!

The American Clock and Watch Museum displayed a Trains, Planes, and Automobiles exhibit in 2016. It featured timepieces associated with transportation.

You might have a **furnace** where you live. It produces heat to keep you warm. The Beckley Furnace was a different kind of furnace. People used it to melt iron. That iron was made into train car wheels.

You can stand inside the furnace if you like. Don't worry. It's not burning anymore! Iron was an important factory product in the 1800s. Today, Connecticut factories still make things with metal. They produce knives, tools, and other metal goods.

Many Connecticut factories make things for the U.S. government. They build submarines, helicopters, and airplane parts. Connecticut makes medicine, soap, and computers, too.

The Beckley Furnace is made of local marble and stands 40 feet (12 m) high!

MASSACHUSETTS

• East Canaan

NEW YORK

RHODE ISLAND

What's Made in Connecticut?
Transportation equipment, machinery, and fabricated metal products

What a blast! I mean, it's a blast furnace. They blasted air in to help the burning process.

John Beckley built the Beckley Furnace in 1847. It operated until 1919 and got as hot as 3,000°F (1,650°C)!

What's Mined In Connecticut?
Crushed stone and sand and gravel

Connecticut's busiest whaling ports were New London, Stonington, and Mystic.

Whale oil was burned in streetlights, lighthouses, and train headlights!

Whale bone was used in clothing to make it stiff.

MASSACHUSETTS

NEW YORK

RHODE ISLAND

Ahoy, mates! We can take a ride on one of the ships at the seaport! Shiver me timbers!

New London •

Mystic
•

Stonington

The Maritime Aquarium is in Norwalk.

• Norwalk

The Mystic Seaport Museum of America and the Sea has historic ships and photographs on display.

You can climb aboard the *Charles W. Morgan* at Mystic. It was the world's last wooden whaling ship.

WHALING DAYS AT MYSTIC SEAPORT

Want to go below deck on a real whaling ship? Then head to Mystic Seaport! It's built just like an old coastal village.

Whaling was a big **industry** in the 1800s. Connecticut had the second-largest whaling industry of all the states. Mystic was known for both whaling and shipbuilding.

Whalers sailed out to sea in big ships. They often stayed out for weeks. The whales they brought back had many uses. Whale blubber, or fat, was made into oil. People burned the oil in lamps.

Check out the Charles W. Morgan, *a whaling ship from the 1800s.*

Do you like farm fairs? Then try the Brooklyn Fair. It started in the 1850s. You've never seen anything like it! It's got a horse-pulling contest. There are working cattle competitions and lawn mower races. There's a contest for dogs, too. The dog with the best tricks gets a prize!

Connecticut doesn't have much farmland. But farmers make the most of it. Some grow shrubs and flowers for people's yards. Some raise dairy cattle for their milk. Others raise chickens that lay eggs. Hay, corn, and tobacco are important crops.

People go fishing for seafood, too. They catch lobsters, oysters, crabs, and clams. Of course, they also catch fish.

Enjoy live music at the Brooklyn Fair.

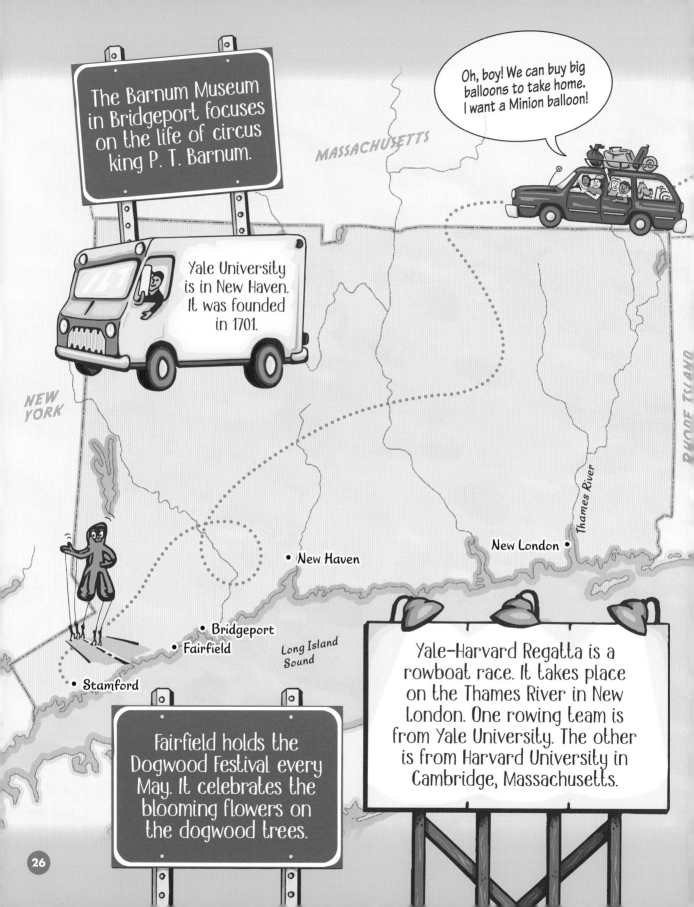

STAMFORD'S GIANT BALLOON PARADE

Here comes Po. There goes Shrek. And there's Scooby-Doo. It's the UBS Parade Spectacular!

Stamford holds this parade close to Thanksgiving. The giant balloons are incredible! They're way above everybody's heads.

You can have plenty of fun in Connecticut. There are boat races and craft shows. In the winter, people enjoy skiing and sleigh rides.

The forests are great for hiking and camping. Some people prefer the seashore. They swim, fish, and collect seashells.

Giant balloons soar over spectators' heads.

Y ou'll love touring the submarine USS *Nautilus*. First, you enter the **torpedo** room. Next, you see where the sailors slept. They had bunk beds, showers, and toilets. Finally, you visit the attack center. That's where sailors spotted targets and fired torpedoes.

The *Nautilus* was the first **nuclear**-powered submarine. It's docked at Groton, where it was built.

Connecticut began building submarines in the 1920s. Business sped up during World War II (1939–1945). Connecticut made many kinds of war supplies. These included submarines, airplane parts, and **ammunition**. Everyone was proud of the USS *Nautilus*. It was first launched in 1954.

Explore the USS Nautilus. *The control room holds the tools used to control the ship.*

The U.S. Navy runs the Naval Submarine Base New London. It is on the Thames River near Groton.

MASSACHUSETTS

NEW YORK

RHODE ISLAND

Thames River

Wow! Look at those torpedoes. They're longer than my bedroom!

New London • • Groton

Groton's Submarine Force Museum is next to the *Nautilus*. It has the world's finest collection of submarine items.

The U.S. Coast Guard Academy moved to New London in 1910.

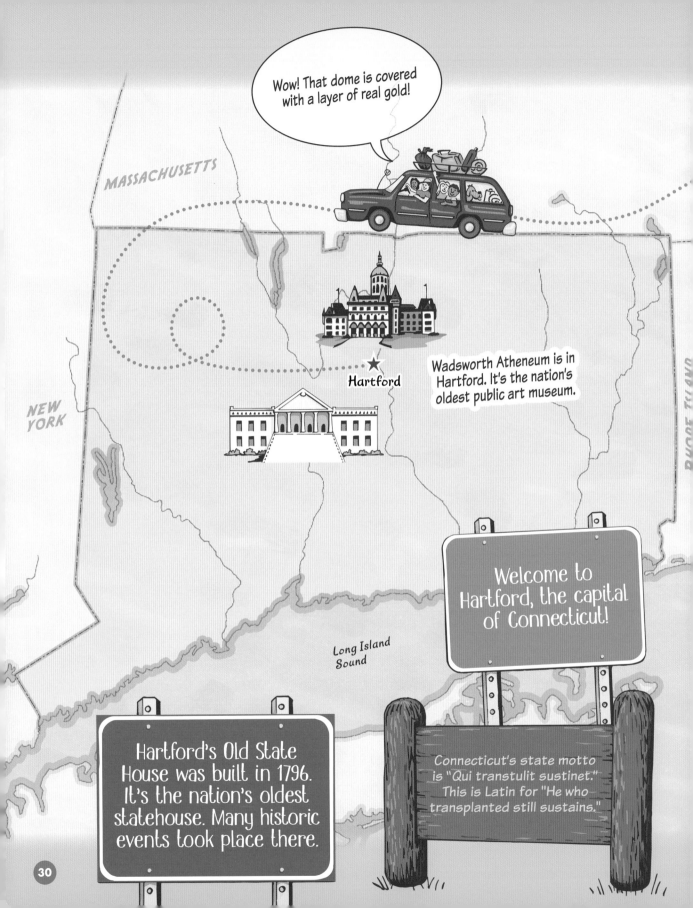

THE STATE CAPITOL IN HARTFORD

The state capitol is very fancy. It looks almost like a castle. Some corners have pointy towers. The tallest tower is in the center. There's a golden dome on top. The dome sparkles in the sunlight!

Many government offices are in the capitol. Connecticut's government has three branches. One branch makes the state's laws. It's called the General Assembly. Another branch carries out those laws. It's headed by the governor. Courts make up the third branch. They decide whether someone has broken the law.

The marble on the capitol's outside walls came from Connecticut.

MARK TWAIN'S HOUSE IN HARTFORD

Windows and chimneys are sticking out everywhere. But where are the doors? It's hard to know where to go in!

This odd house belonged to author Mark Twain. He wrote many books there. One was *The Adventures of Tom Sawyer.* Another was *The Adventures of Huckleberry Finn.* Even today, people still enjoy these stories. They show how children might have lived long ago.

Noah Webster was another famous person from Connecticut. He put together the first dictionary. It had thousands of words in it!

Twain lived in the Hartford house from 1874 to 1891.

Mark Twain's real name was Samuel Langhorne Clemens.

The first public library in Connecticut opened in New Haven in 1656.

MASSACHUSETTS

NEW YORK

RHODE ISLAND

What's that house shaped like? An L? An S? I can't tell!

West Hartford

★ Hartford

New Haven

Dear Mr. Twain:
Thanks for writing about Tom Sawyer. He was always getting into trouble. But he was really a good kid. Maybe there's hope for me, too!

Sincerely,
A. Book Worm

post card

Mark Twain
1835-1910
Hartford, CT

Noah Webster (1758-1843) was born in West Hartford. You can tour his home there.

Webster's *American Dictionary of the English Language* was first published in 1828.

MASSACHUSETTS

NEW YORK

RHODE ISLAND

Look! Up in the sky! It's a Pteranodon!

• Rocky Hill

Pteranodon was a flying reptile. Its name means "winged and toothless."

• New Haven

Long Island Sound

Check out Dinosaur State Park in Rocky Hill. You'll see dinosaur footprints there. They're about 200 million years old!

Some of the dinosaur skeletons at the Peabody Museum were among the first found in North America.

DINOSAURS AT THE PEABODY MUSEUM

How big were dinosaurs? Try walking around in a room full of them. Just visit the Yale Peabody Museum of Natural History. It's at Yale University in New Haven.

The Peabody Museum's Great Hall of Dinosaurs is awesome. Dinosaur skeletons are everywhere. You'll see just how big some of those monsters were. You'd barely come up to their knees!

You'll also see saber-toothed cats. They had long, pointy teeth. There are skeletons of early humans, too. They're closer to your size!

A triceratops greets visitors to the Yale Peabody Museum of Natural History.

OUR TRIP

We visited many amazing places on our trip! We also met a lot of interesting people along the way. Look at the map below. Use your finger to trace all the places we have been.

Where is Heublein Tower located? *See page 6 for the answer.*

How many toes do black bears have on each foot? *Page 9 has the answer.*

Who fought in the Pequot War? *See page 10 for the answer.*

How old was Nathan Hale when he died? *Look on page 13 for the answer.*

Who is a steerperson? *Page 17 has the answer.*

How hot did the Beckley Furnace get? *Turn to page 21 for the answer.*

What is the name of the last wooden whale ship? *Look on page 22 and find out!*

What can you see in the Yale-Harvard Regatta? *Turn to page 26 for the answer.*

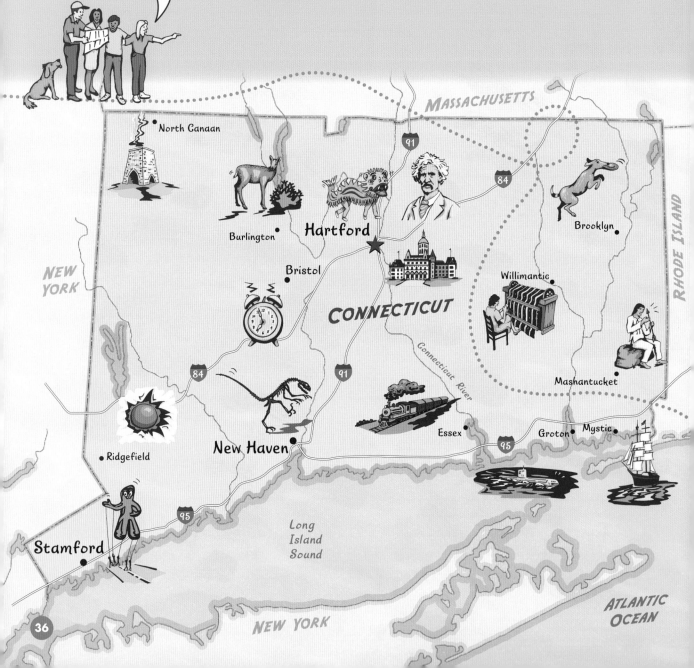

State flag

State seal

STATE SYMBOLS

State animal: Sperm whale

State bird: American robin

State composer: Charles Ives

State flower: Mountain laurel

State folk dance: Square dance

State fossil: Eubrontes giganteus

State hero: Nathan Hale

State heroine: Prudence Crandall

State insect: European mantis (praying mantis)

State mineral: Garnet

State shellfish: Eastern oyster

State ship: USS *Nautilus*

State tree: Charter oak (White oak)

STATE SONG

"YANKEE DOODLE"

Traditional words and music

Yankee Doodle went to town,
Riding on a pony,
Stuck a feather in his hat,
And called it macaroni.

Chorus:
Yankee Doodle keep it up,
Yankee Doodle dandy,
Mind the music and the step,
And with the folks be handy.

That was a great trip! We traveled all over Connecticut!
There are a few places that we didn't have time for, though. Next time, we plan to visit Louis' Lunch in New Haven. The first hamburger was served there in 1900. You can still enjoy a juicy burger there today.

FAMOUS PEOPLE

Arnold, Benedict (1741–1801), army officer, traitor

Bacon, Kevin (1958–), actor who lives in Connecticut

Barnum, P. T. (1810–1891), showman

Brown, John (1800–1859), abolitionist

Bush, George W. (1946–), 43rd U.S. president

Collins, Suzanne (1962–), author

Colt, Samuel (1814–1862), inventor

Goodyear, Charles (1800–1860), inventor

Grasso, Ella (1919–1981), first woman elected governor of a state

Hale, Nathan (1755–1776), American Revolutionary War hero

Hamill, Dorothy (1956–), figure skater

Hepburn, Katharine (1907–2003), actor

Mayer, John (1977–), singer, songwriter, and musician

Sendak, Maurice (1928–2012), artist

Stowe, Harriet Beecher (1811–1896), author

Trumbull, Johnathan, Sr. (1710–1785), merchant and politician

Twain, Mark (1835–1910), author

Tyson, Mike (1966–), boxer

Webster, Noah (1758–1843), author of first American dictionary

Whitney, Eli (1765–1825), inventor

WORDS TO KNOW

ammunition (am-yuh-NISH-uhn) objects such as bullets that are fired from guns

colonists (KOL-uh-nists) people who settle in a new land that is controlled by their home country

colony (KOL-uh-nee) a land with ties to a mother country

furnace (FUR-niss) a machine that burns fuel to create heat

immigrants (IM-uh-gruhnts) people who leave their home country and move to another land

industry (IN-duh-stree) a type of business

nuclear (NOO-klee-ur) having to do with the energy inside tiny particles called atoms

tavern (TAV-urn) a public house where people can eat and drink

torpedo (tor-PEE-doh) an underwater weapon fired from a submarine

TO LEARN MORE

IN THE LIBRARY

Boehme, Gerry. *Connecticut*. New York, NY: Cavendish Square Publishing, 2015.

Cunningham, Kevin. *The Connecticut Colony*. New York, NY: Children's Press, 2012.

Koontz, Robin. *Connecticut: The Constitution State*. New York, NY: PowerKids Press, 2011.

ON THE WEB

Visit our Web site for links about Connecticut:

childsworld.com/links

Note to Parents, Teachers, and Librarians: We routinely verify our Web links to make sure they are safe and active sites. So encourage your readers to check them out!

PLACES TO VISIT OR CONTACT

The Connecticut Historical Society

chs.org

One Elizabeth Street

Hartford, CT 06105

860/236-5621

For more information about the history of Connecticut

Connecticut Office of Tourism

ctvisit.com

One Constitution Plaza, 2nd Floor

Hartford, CT 06103

860/256-2800

For more information about traveling in Connecticut

Connecticut covers 5,543 square miles (14,357 sq km). It's the 48th-largest state in size.

INDEX

Bye, Constitution State.
We had a great time.
We'll come back soon!